THE FRENCH LANDSCAPE
IMAGES OF A SPECIAL LIGHT

What people are saying about "The French Landscape"

When your book is published I am going to buy a coffee table to put under it.
– Gretchen, New York City, NY

Your work is magnificent. Regardless of the photographic tool, the eye of the artist show! Absolutely wonderful images. In the grand tradition of the great black and white photographers—with a special flair.
– Dale, Menlo Park, CA

I thought of you today as I went into the Grand Palais for the first time since the renovations were complete. I'd love to see your infrared work of Paris.
– Sylvia, Paris, France

Randy, your black and white photographs popped up on the Paris page today. They're so beautiful! I await your book with even more anticipation—I can see why you are titling it the way you are.
– Dawn, Baltimore, Maryland

Your infrared take on the world is just too darn unique to be ignored.
– Stuart, Belmont, CA

I'm very impressed by your photographs, especially your feeling for light.
– Emma, Lund, Sweden

This book is destined to be a great success—especially among us Paris lovers.
– Gayle, Boston, MA

The photographs are beautiful. The angles, shadows and perspective are really wonderful. I'll look for your book in the future—I'm sure it will be fantastic.
– Crown, Ontario, Canada

I too, will have a spot for your book when it comes out, right next to "Paris Then and Now." Can't wait, what beautiful, beautiful photographs.
— Satchel, San Francisco, CA

THE FRENCH LANDSCAPE

IMAGES OF A SPECIAL LIGHT

RANDY SILVER

I would like to dedicate this book
to the three women in my life;
my wife Anne, daughter Erica
and granddaughter Lucy.

TABLE OF CONTENTS

FOREWORD

Black & White photography has been a fascinating and interesting medium and has not diminished since the first permanent photograph was made in 1826 by the French inventor Nicéphore Niépce. Louis Daguerre, working in collaboration, later perfected the daguerreotype.

Fast forward a few years and you have Kodak developing a special film used for Aerial, Photographic Surveillance, Medical and evidence photography. This film was called Infrared film and was used to record beyond the visible spectrum. It recorded images in a spectrum that the human eye could not see, that is, until the film was developed and a print was made.

This film, along with its extraordinary characteristics, had its special requirements. Kodak B&W High Speed Infrared was the most sensitive to capture the 700 to 900 nanometers range - or the near infrared range.

I remember seeing the first images in B&W infrared and I was astounded at not only their beauty, but how infrared added a feeling of mystery and romance to the image. And so, I became hooked. I learned all I could about this film and soon began using it.

I used it almost exclusively outdoors and in a beautiful scenic setting; looking for the most attractive area that would lend itself even more spectacular with the use of infrared film. It would render that mystical, romantic and surreal look I was hoping to get.

Black & White infrared photography takes photography to a different realm. It has a quality all its own and there is nothing else photographically like it, especially when Kodak High Speed Infrared film was used. And that's what makes the images so exciting.

Randy Silver, armed with his Nikons and a few select Nikon lenses, took off for France to photograph the beautiful French Landscape. Randy has been actively using infrared film for almost 20 years and traveled to photograph extensively all over the world. His travels have taken him throughout the US, Canada, England, Scotland, Wales, Ireland, Holland, Germany, Austria, Hungary, Russia and China.

Not only has Randy had a successful photography business for almost 40 years, he also has had a busy schedule in teaching photography classes and workshops.

In fact, it was after one of these workshops that the trip to France materialized. At first Randy was a little hesitant and thought the French people would be rude and stand offish. But, after 20 minutes in Paris that myth was dispelled. He knew he would return again and again; in fact four more times. Each time in September when the light for photography is just gorgeous.

So Randy set about photographing the French Landscape; his photographic journeys took him to Paris, Normandy, Brittany, the Dordogne, Loire Valley and Burgundy.

Having extensive experience in photography, he combined that experience with his understanding of light and composition. This, along with his passion for photography is what gives his special photographs that dreamlike quality that seems to add the dimension of depth to his photographs. That was the first thing I noticed about Randy's photographs, how they appear to be almost three dimensional.

After capturing these beautiful images over a five year period, the framework for the book was conceived. What started as a visit to France turned into a passion lasting for years as he photographed the French Landscape... in a Special Light.

Ferdinand Neubauer
Master Photographer and Author
Adventures in Infrared

PREFACE

This book came about in an indirect way. I had taught classes in the United States and workshops in a number of countries. During those times, my wife Anne, had served as chief cook and bottle washer. By 2000 it was time for her to have a genuine vacation where she could choose the destination. France it was in 2000 and was followed by 4 subsequent trips throughout Paris, Normandy, Brittany, the Dordogne and Burgundy. Included were barge trips on 3 different rivers/canals and two hot air balloon adventures.

There was so much to photograph on the French Landscape—vineyards, chateaus, meandering rivers, historical buildings and livestock. As a photographer I was at first overwhelmed. Everywhere I looked I saw striking features on the landscape.

Often, when people see my images, the first thing said is "what kind of camera did you use?" There is often the thought that it must have been taken with the latest "state of the art" equipment. Let me clarify, all of the images in this book were taken with a Nikon FE 2 and a Nikon F (that I purchased in Paris). All of the images were also taken hand-held. For those who know the equipment, when the Nikon F gives up the ghost, I am going down to the marina and sell it as an anchor.

In teaching photography for over 30 years, it has always a pleasure to observe students as they have an "ah ha" experience. They begin to understand and pay attention to the image being mostly in their physical and emotion response, somewhat on the landscape and very little in the camera.

When I began using infrared almost 20 years ago, it was a medium that permitted me to explore the landscape in a new way, taking photographs with light I couldn't see. The "ah ha" experience got a hold of me once more.

Why infrared? Its been described as dramatic and breathtaking, surreal, mystical with shimmering highlights and soft, delicate dreamlike auras. It renders landscapes and architectural photographs bold and unusual.

It's difficult to imagine what goes on with a photographer on the Seine, in the Latin Quarter, near Notre Dame, Montmartre or Pere Lachaise Cemetery, unless you are there. They will never be the same. The images will dance around in their head; hopefully in their camera as well. If you ask them about their photography experience in France, the response might be: "Even if I had the words to tell you, you might not have the ears to hear it."

Security issues have made it almost impossible to travel with Kodak High Speed Infrared film (2481). The film box and canister say "Load, Unload and Process In Total Darkness." TSA personnel and other security staff are unwilling to allow hand inspection or will want to open the boxes and canisters, thus ruining the film.

Through a series of procedures, a type of infrared image can now be obtained with a digital camera. The future of traveling and capturing infrared images will be done with digital equipment.

I hope you enjoy the journey into B&W infrared. It's all there for you as you explore the world beyond the visible spectrum.

BIOGRAPHY

Following in the footsteps of the first two professional photographers in his family, his grandfather and mother, Randy began his career in 1969.

Having taught photography throughout the United States and Canada, he embarked on workshops in the British Isles and Ireland. His work in infrared photography has been featured in numerous magazines as well as one person exhibits in the greater San Francisco area.

Since 2000, he has photographed in France, China, Tibet, The Netherlands, Germany, Austria, Hungary and Russia.

He lives with his wife Anne and dachshund Meg in Northern California.

ACKNOWLEDGMENTS

Portia Steele, who became my agent, conceived the idea of a book from my images and convinced me to work in that direction.

Sherman Hines and his design and production staff who helped me bring life to the concept.

Photographer Ferdinand Neubauer from North Carolina who was kind to review the images and write the forward.

And to my close friend and fellow photographer Hagop Istanboulian who has worked with me technically and creatively for the past 14 years.

Paris Skyline I

Paris Skyline II

Eiffel Tower I

Eiffel Tower II

IM Pei Glass Pyramid

The Louvre (Old and New)

From the 5th Arrondissement
to Notre Dame

Tuillieries

Laid Back
Tuillieries

Luxembourg Gardens

Fountaine de Medicis
Luxembourg Gardens

Contemplation
Art in the Park

Footsteps along the Seine

Pont Alexandre III

On the Waterway

Canal St-Martin

Fountain at Place de la Concorde

Notre Dame Cathedral

Honored at the Arc de Triomphe

Gazing Upward at Invalides

Saint-Sulpice Church

Carnavalet

Globes at Palais Royal

Buren Columns at Palais Royal

Les Bouquinistes

Birdman of Sacre-Coeur

Burgers of Calais – Rodin

Gates of Hell – Rodin

From Rodin to Invalides

Rodin sculpture and Invalides

Pere Lachaise Cemetery I

Pere Lachaise Cemetery II

Pere Lachaise Cemetery III

La Grande Arche
La Défense

At La Défense

Monet's Garden I
Giverny

Shadow Basilique Ste Madeleine
Vezelay

Shadow Basilique Ste Madeleine
Vezelay

Monet's Garden II
Giverny

St-Malo
Brittany

Cloisters Mont-St-Michel
Normandy

Mulberry Harbour Remains
Arromanches

Not Forgotten – American Cemetery
Coleville

One of Many – American Cemetery
Coleville

Cadouin Abbey 1115 AD
Perigord

Courtyard Cadouin Abbey
Perigord

Leaves and Shadows
Quimper

Prehistoric Structure
Brittany

A Quiet Place
Dijon

Roman Amphitheater
Lyon

Choregraphie
Lyon

Basilique Notre Dame de Fourviere
Lyon

Village Square
Perouges

Ripples
Nivernais Canal

At the Quay
Benyac

Waiting
On the Soane

Barge in the Mist

Bridge
Near Auxerre

On the Loire Canal

Infinity
Loire Canal

Balloon
Over the Nivernais

Balloon
Over the Loire Valley

Vineyards
Chablis

View
Above Burgundy

Chateau Villandry
Loire Valley

Chateau Chenenceau
Loire Valley

Rance River
Dinan

Ancient Bridge

Wooden Curtain
Dordogne

Hayfield
Dordogne

Art in Architecture
Dordogne

From High on
Chateau Biron

The Dordogne River

A Bridge Afar
Dordogne River

Village from Chateau Biron
Dordogne

Rocamador
Dordogne

Chateau Hautefort I
Dordogne

Chateau Hautefort II
Dordogne

The Turret

Gardens of the Manor Eyrignac
Dordogne

INDEX

Print run of this volume is 1000 limited edition
Published by: R S Silver and Light

R S Silver and Light
P.O. Box 6894
San Carlos, CA 94070
randy-silver-photo@juno.com

Printed in China